INTRODUCTION

The ability to sight-read fluently is a most important part of your training as a recorder player. Yet the *study* of sight-reading is often badly neglected by young players and is frequently regarded as no more than a rather unpleasant side-line. If you become a *good* sight-reader you will be able to learn pieces more quickly, and play in ensembles with confidence and assurance. Also, in grade examinations, good performance in the sight-reading test will result in useful extra marks!

The author wishes to thank Sally Adams for many helpful suggestions.

Using the workbook

The purpose of this workbook is to incorporate sight-reading regularly into your practice and lessons, and to help you prepare for the sight-reading test in grade examinations. It offers you a progressive series of enjoyable and stimulating stages in which, with careful work, you should show considerable improvement from week to week.

Each stage consists of two parts: firstly, exercises which you should prepare in advance, along with a short piece with questions; and secondly, an unprepared test, to be found at the end of the book.

Your teacher will mark your work according to accuracy. Each stage carries a maximum of 50 marks and your work will be assessed as follows:

> 2 marks for each of the six questions relating to the prepared piece (total 12).
> 18 marks for the prepared piece itself.
> 20 marks for the unprepared test. (Teachers should devise a similar series of questions for the unprepared test, and take the answers into account when allocating a final mark.)

Space is given at the end of each stage for you to keep a running total of your marks as you progress. If you are scoring 40 or more each time you are doing well!

At the top of the first page in each stage you will see one or two new features to be introduced. There are then normally four different types of exercise:

1 **Rhythmic exercises** It is very important that you should be able to feel and maintain a steady beat. These exercises will help develop this ability. There are at least four ways of doing these exercises: clap or tap the lower line (the beat) while singing the upper line to 'la'; tap the lower line with your foot and clap the upper line; on a table or flat surface, tap the lower line with one hand and the upper line with the other; 'play' the lower line on a metronome and clap or tap the upper line.

2 **Melodic exercises** Fluent sight-reading depends on recognising melodic shapes at first glance. These shapes are often related to scales and arpeggios. Before you begin, always notice the *key-signature* and the notes affected by it, along with any accidentals.

3 **A prepared piece with questions** You should prepare carefully both the piece and the questions, which are to help you think about and understand the piece before you play it. Put your answers in the spaces provided.

4 **An unprepared piece** Finally, your teacher will give you an *unprepared* test to be read at *sight*. Make sure you have read the *Sight-reading Checklist* on page 23 before you begin each piece.

Remember to count throughout each piece and to keep going at a steady and even tempo. Always try to look ahead, at least to the next note or beat.

NAME		
EXAMINATION RECORD		
GRADE	DATE	MARK

(handwritten, top right)
1–3 Grade 1
4–7 " 2
8–10 " 3

TEACHER'S NAME	
TELEPHONE	

©1993 by Faber Music Ltd
First published in 1993 by Faber Music Ltd
3 Queen Square, London WC1N 3AU
Design and typography by James Butler
Cover design by M & S Tucker
Music and text set by Silverfen
Printed in England

Improve your Sight-reading! Grades I-V

Violin I	ISBN	0 571 51385 9
Violin II	ISBN	0 571 51386 7
Violin III	ISBN	0 571 51387 5
Violin IV	ISBN	0 571 51388 3
Violin V	ISBN	0 571 51389 1
Violin Supplement	ISBN	0 571 51167 8
Viola	ISBN	0 571 51075 2
Cello	ISBN	0 571 51027 2
Double bass	ISBN	0 571 51149 X
Descant recorder I-III	ISBN	0 571 51373 5
Flute	ISBN	0 571 51025 6
Oboe	ISBN	0 571 51026 4
Clarinet	ISBN	0 571 50983 5
Saxophone	ISBN	0 571 51074 4
Bassoon	ISBN	0 571 51148 1
Horn	ISBN	0 571 51076 0
Trumpet	ISBN	0 571 50989 4
Trombone/Euphonium	ISBN	0 571 51077 9
Piano I	ISBN	0 571 51241 0
Piano II	ISBN	0 571 51242 9
Piano III	ISBN	0 571 51243 7
Piano IV	ISBN	0 571 51244 5
Piano V	ISBN	0 571 51245 3

Improve your Sight-reading! Grades V-VIII

Piano VI	ISBN	0 571 51330 1
Piano VII	ISBN	0 571 51331 X
Piano VIII	ISBN	0 571 51332 8
Violin	ISBN	0 571 51153 8
Flute	ISBN	0 571 51150 3
Clarinet	ISBN	0 571 51151 1
Trumpet	ISBN	0 571 51152 X

STAGE 1

C major

RHYTHMIC EXERCISES

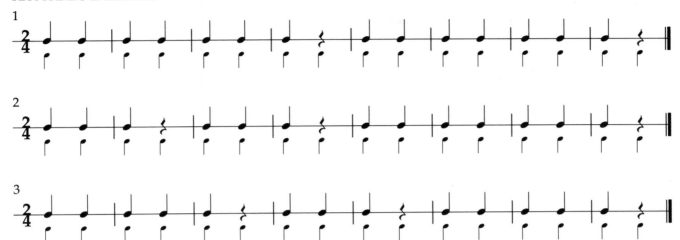

MELODIC EXERCISES

This music is copyright. Photocopying is illegal.

PREPARED PIECE

	Marks*
1 What does *Moderato* mean?	☐
2 What will you count?	☐
3 What does *mf* mean?	☐
4 What are the letter names of the first three notes?	☐
5 What is the rest in bar two called?	☐
6 What is the duration of the rest?	☐
Total:	☐

Unprepared tests page 23

Mark: ☐

Prepared work total: ☐

Unprepared: ☐

Total: ☐

*The mark boxes are to be filled in by your teacher (see Introduction).

STAGE 2

RHYTHMIC EXERCISES

1

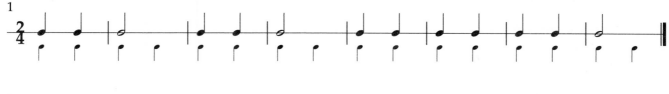

2

3

MELODIC EXERCISES

1

2

3

PREPARED PIECE

1   How many beats are there in each bar?

2   In which key is the piece written?

3   How many beats is each crotchet (♩) worth?

4   How many beats is each minim (♩) worth?

5   What does *Allegretto* mean?

6   What does *f (forte)* indicate?

Total:

Unprepared tests page 24

Mark:

Prepared work total:

Unprepared:

Total:

Running totals:

1   2

STAGE 3

Slurs 4
4
G major

RHYTHMIC EXERCISES

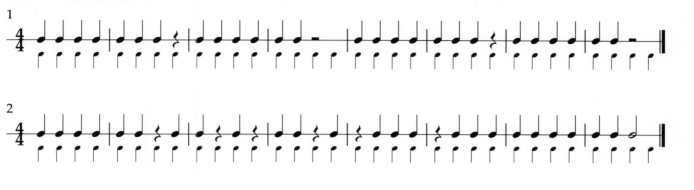

1

2

3

MELODIC EXERCISES

1

2

3

4

PREPARED PIECE

1 What does $\frac{4}{4}$ indicate? How many beats will you count in each bar? ✓

2 What does ⌣ indicate? ✓

3 How many beats is each crotchet rest (𝄽) worth? ✓

4 What are the letter names of the notes in the first bar? ✓

5 What does *f (forte)* indicate? ✓

6 What is the meaning of *Allegretto*?

Total:

Allegro

Allegretto

f

5

p

9

f

Unprepared tests page 25   Mark: ✓

Prepared work total:

Unprepared:

Total:

Running totals:

1	2	3

STAGE 4 Grade 2

$\frac{3}{4}$ **F major**

RHYTHMIC EXERCISES

1

2

3

MELODIC EXERCISES

1

2

3

4

PREPARED PIECE

1   What does $\frac{3}{4}$ indicate?

2   How many beats is each minim (♩) worth?

3   How many beats is the dotted minim (♩.) worth?

4   What is the letter name of the first note in bar 2?

5   What does **mf** (*mezzo-forte*) indicate?

6   What is the meaning of *Andante*?

Total:

Andante

mf

6

11

Unprepared tests page 26   Mark:

Prepared work total:

Unprepared:

Total:

Running totals:

1	2	3	4

STAGE 5

D major
Staccato

RHYTHMIC EXERCISES

MELODIC EXERCISES

PREPARED PIECE

1 What does $\frac{4}{4}$ indicate?

2 Clap the following rhythms:

3 What does *p* indicate?

4 What does *mf* indicate?

5 What does ⟨ indicate?

6 What is the meaning of *Allegro moderato*?

Total:

Allegro moderato

Unprepared tests page 27

Mark:

Prepared work total:

Unprepared:

Total:

Running totals:

1	2	3	4	5

STAGE 6

A minor
Simple tied notes

RHYTHMIC EXERCISES

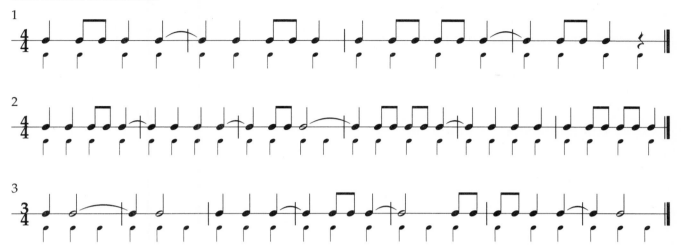

MELODIC EXERCISES

PREPARED PIECE

1　In which key is this piece written?

2　What is the letter name of the last note in bar 2?

3　How many beats are there in each bar?

4　Why are there so many F♯s and G♯s in this piece?

5　What is the meaning of *Moderato con moto*?

6　What do *dim. (diminuendo)* and *cresc. (crescendo)* indicate?

Total:

Unprepared tests page 28

Mark:

Prepared work total:

Unprepared:

Total:

Running totals:

1	2	3	4	5	6

STAGE 7

RHYTHMIC EXERCISES

1

2

3

MELODIC EXERCISES

1

2

3

4

PREPARED PIECE

1 In which key is this piece written?

2 What does *Andante con moto* mean?

3 What will you count?

4 What are the letter names of the notes in bar seven?

5 What does the marking ♩ ♩ indicate?

6 What does *cresc.* mean?

Total:

Andante con moto

Unprepared tests page 29

Mark:

Prepared work total:

Unprepared:

Total:

Running totals:

1	2	3	4	5	6	7

STAGE 8

D minor

RHYTHMIC EXERCISES

MELODIC EXERCISES

PREPARED PIECE

1 How many beats are there in each bar?

2 In which key is the piece written?

3 Do you think this is a happy or sad piece?

4 Mark the first note affected by the key-signature.

5 What are the letter names of the notes in bar seven?

6 What does *rall. (rallentando)* mean?

Total:

Unprepared tests page 30

Mark:

Prepared work total:

Unprepared:

Total:

Running totals:

1	2	3	4	5	6	7	8

STAGE 9

RHYTHMIC EXERCISES

1

2

3

MELODIC EXERCISES

1

2

3

PREPARED PIECE

1 How many beats are there in each bar?

2 Mark the accidental with a cross.

3 What does *mf* indicate?

4 What does the marking ♩ indicate?

5 What is the meaning of *Andante, tempo di minuetto*?

6 Clap this rhythm:

Total:

Andante, tempo di minuetto

Unprepared tests page 31

Mark:

Prepared work total:

Unprepared:

Total:

Running totals:

1	2	3	4	5	6	7	8	9

STAGE 10

RHYTHMIC EXERCISES

MELODIC EXERCISES

PREPARED PIECE

1 In which key is the piece written?

2 How many beats are there in each bar?

3 Mark the note affected by the key-signature.

4 Mark with a bracket two bars in which the arpeggio of G major occurs.

5 What does *Allegro giocoso* mean?

6 Clap this rhythm:

Total:

Allegro giocoso

Unprepared tests page 32

Mark:

Prepared work total:

Unprepared:

Total:

Running totals:

1	2	3	4	5	6	7	8	9	10

CONCLUSION

A sight-reading checklist

Before you begin to play a piece at sight, always remember to consider the following:

1   Look at the key-signature, and find the notes which need raising or lowering.

2   Look at the time-signature, and decide how you will count the piece.

3   Notice any accidentals that may occur.

4   Notice scale and arpeggio patterns.

5   Work out leger-line notes if necessary.

6   Notice dynamic and other markings.

7   Look at the tempo mark and decide what speed to play.

8   Count one bar before you begin, to establish the speed.

When performing your sight-reading piece, always remember to:

1   CONTINUE TO COUNT THROUGHOUT THE PIECE.

2   Keep going at a steady and even tempo.

3   Ignore mistakes.

4   Check the key-signature at the beginning of each new line.

5   Look ahead – at least to the next beat or note.

6   Play *musically*.

UNPREPARED TESTS
STAGE 1

3   Andante

STAGE 2

1   Moderato

2   Andante

3   Allegretto

STAGE 3

1   Allegretto

2   Moderato

3   Andante con moto

STAGE 4

1   Allegro moderato

2   Andante

3   Allegretto

STAGE 5

1   Andante con moto

2   Allegro moderato

3   Allegretto

STAGE 6

1   Andante cantabile

2   Allegretto scherzando

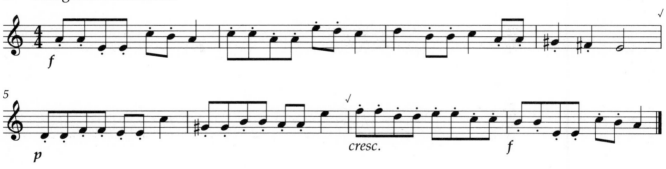

3   Alla gavotta

STAGE 7

1   Andante

2   Animato

3   Allegretto

STAGE 8

1 Andante

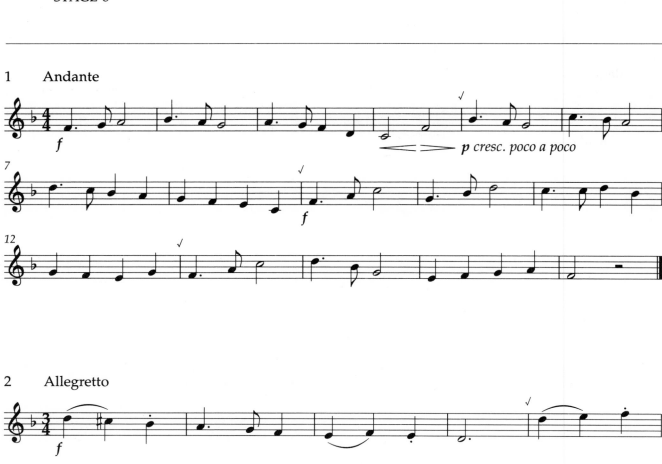

2 Allegretto

3 Alla marcia

STAGE 9

STAGE 10

1 Allegro

2 Andante con moto

3 Allegro

* The high C can be fingered: